A Simple Guide

to

Finding a Job with LinkedIn™

by
Claire Hunter and
Michele Somody

LUMINIS BOOKS
Published by Luminis Books
1950 East Greyhound Pass, #18, PMB 280
Carmel, Indiana, 46033, U.S.A.
Copyright © Luminis Books, 2013

PUBLISHER'S NOTICE

Cover art direction and design by Luminis Books. Cover photo courtesy of Shutterstock.

ISBN-10: 1-935462-78-4
ISBN-13: 978-1-935462-78-1
Printed in the United States of America

10 9 8 7 6 5 4 3 2 1

Simple Guides

give you

Just the Facts

Get up to speed with LinkedIn—fast!

Simple Guides: get you started quickly.

No extra clutter, no extra reading.

Learn how to **set up your profile in LinkedIn,** as well as how to **manage your HomePage and add professional contacts.**

Find out about all the features of LinkedIn, how to **provide links to websites and blogs, add photos, signatures and build your network.**

Learn about all the different things you can do to **get recommendations, contact prospective employers, send your resume, search for new jobs, and find the job you want!**

From Claire: Thanks for the support of my wonderful family. You're always there!

From Michele: Thank you to my loving husband Bob and my children Faithe and Brian.

Table of Contents

Chapter 1

Getting to Know LinkedIn

LinkedIn is the world's largest professional network on the Internet. LinkedIn has more than 150 million members in over 200 countries. More than 60% of LinkedIn members are from outside of the United States. It is available in 16 languages:

- ➢ English
- ➢ Czech
- ➢ Dutch
- ➢ French
- ➢ German
- ➢ Indonesian
- ➢ Italian
- ➢ Japanese

- ➢ Korean
- ➢ Malay
- ➢ Portuguese
- ➢ Romanian
- ➢ Russian
- ➢ Spanish
- ➢ Swedish
- ➢ Turkish

Figure 1-1: LinkedIn is the world's largest professional network on the Internet.

LinkedIn allows you to connect to other trusted professionals to exchange ideas and experiences.

The History of LinkedIn

LinkedIn was co-founded by Reid Hoffman in 2002. The LinkedIn site was launched in May 2003. It is a publicly held company traded on the New York Stock Exchange (LNKD). LinkedIn's management team includes executives from Yahoo!, Microsoft, Google, and other well-known companies.

More than two new members sign up every second. Students and recent graduates are the fastest growing demographic in LinkedIn.

Mobile Versions of LinkedIn

LinkedIn's free applications for BlackBerry and iPhone allow you to be connected from wherever you may be. The mobile versions have reduced features and are available in only six languages:

- Chinese
- English
- French
- German
- Japanese
- Spanish

The BlackBerry application features:

- Network Updates
- Search
- Connections

- ➢ Messages
- ➢ Reconnect

LinkedIn's iPhone application can be downloaded for free from iTunes.

Figure 1-2: LinkedIn for the iPhone can be downloaded for free from iTunes.

LinkedIn's iPhone application features:

- ➢ Search
- ➢ Invite
- ➢ Updates
- ➢ Connections
- ➢ Favorites

- ➢ Inbox and Invitations
- ➢ Recents
- ➢ Reconnect
- ➢ In Person
- ➢ Themes

Top 10 Reasons to Use LinkedIn

1. Keep up-to-date in your industry.
2. Keep in touch with colleagues and clients.
3. Position yourself as an expert.
4. Learn from your network.
5. Recruiters use it to find qualified job candidates.
6. Stimulate discussions.
7. Look for a job.
8. Receive recommendations from your connections.
9. Seek advice from your connections.
10. Everyone is on it!

Just the Facts About LinkedIn

- ➢ LinkedIn is the world's largest professional network on the Internet with more than 150 million members worldwide.
- ➢ LinkedIn is available in 16 languages.
- ➢ LinkedIn offers mobile versions for the iPhone and BlackBerry, with limited features. Mobile versions are available in six languages.

Chapter 2

Getting Started with LinkedIn

In order to use LinkedIn, you need to create an account and become a member. You simply need the following:

- ➢ A computer
- ➢ Access to the Internet
- ➢ A valid e-mail account

How Do I Set Up an Account for LinkedIn?

In order to begin using LinkedIn, you need to set up an account. Setting up an account is free and takes less than two minutes. To set up an account:

1. Go to www.linkedin.com.
2. Enter your First Name and Last Name.
3. Enter your email address.
4. Enter a password with at least 6 characters.
5. Click Join.

Figure 2-1: Setting up a LinkedIn account is free and fast.

You will then begin to set up your profile with a few simple questions. Your profile is very important because it is how you connect with people in your network and how people find you.

Figure 2-2: Your profile is how you connect and network with other professionals.

To continue, you must confirm your email address. Go to your inbox and open the LinkedIn Email Confirmation email. Follow the directions to confirm your email address.

Figure 2-3: Confirm your email address.

After confirming your email address, you must sign in again using your email address and password. You will now come to a screen suggesting some people you may know. Skip this step for now. This will be covered in a later chapter.

Just the Facts About Getting Started with LinkedIn

> ➤ To begin using LinkedIn, you need to set up an account.
> ➤ A LinkedIn account is quick to set up, and it is free.
> ➤ Your profile is very important because it is how you connect with people in your network and how people find you.

Chapter 3

Editing Your Profile

Your profile is the place to showcase your skills and experience. Think of your LinkedIn Profile as your online resume where you can highlight your qualifications, experience, and skills. It allows other professionals to connect, collaborate, and communicate with you.

A complete profile includes:

- ➢ A professional photo
- ➢ Executive Summary
- ➢ Skill Sets
- ➢ Three recent positions
- ➢ Three recommendations from connections

How to Edit Your Profile

To begin, from the Profile drop down menu, select Edit Profile.

Figure 3-1: Edit your profile.

Your profile is the place to showcase your skills and experience. First, upload a professional photo. To do this, browse your computer for an appropriate picture. Note: the file size limit is 4 MB. Upload the photo (this may take a few minutes).

You must decide if you want your profile accessible to My Connections, My Network, or Everyone. It is suggested to make your profile public so that more professionals can find you. Remember, you can always edit your profile at any time.

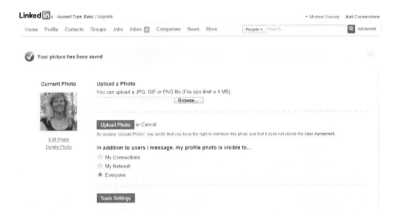

Figure 3-2: Upload a professional photo.

Next, update your basic information. Your basic information is a snapshot of who you are. Your professional headline defaults to your current job title. However, you can customize the headline to attract more opportunities.

Be sure to include your zip code, industry, and maiden name so people can reach out to you with opportunities.

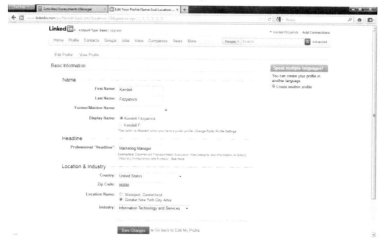

Figure 3-3: Your basic information is a snapshot of who you are.

The Summary section is where you highlight your experience, identify your skill set, and identify accomplishments.

Summary Edit

Responsible for overall charge of a project including planning, direction, implementation, and control. Delegate tasks, manage budgets, meet deadlines, and ensure consistency of project execution with company policies.

Figure 3-4: Highlight your experience in the Summary section.

The Experience section includes your employment history. Be sure to include at least three recent positions and a description of responsibilities and specific accomplishments in these positions.

Figure 3-5: Include both current and past positions in the Experience section.

The Skills & Expertise section allows you to include up to 50 skills that describe your skill set and experience. This is an easy way for recruiters to search for specific skills.

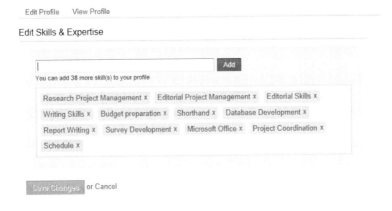

Figure 3-6: Include up to 50 skills.

Recommendations are important because they provide an overview of your strengths. You can choose which recommendations to display. To have a complete profile, you need at least three recommendations. You can ask colleagues to endorse you by writing a recommendation.

Figure 3-7: You need at least three recommendations for a complete profile.

The Additional Information section allows you to add links to personal websites or blogs, list groups and associations, and highlight any honors or awards. Additional information helps professionals find you in keyword searches.

Additional Information

Websites:	+ Add
Twitter:	+ Add
Interests:	+ Add
Groups and Associations:	+ Add
Honors and Awards:	+ Add

Personal Information Edit

Phone:	+ Add
Address:	+ Add
IM:	+ Add
Birthday:	+ Add
Marital status:	+ Add

Figure 3-8: Additional information is helpful in keyword searches.

According to LinkedIn, the top 10 most overused buzzwords used in LinkedIn profiles are:

1. Extensive experience
2. Innovative
3. Team player
4. Motivated
5. Results-oriented
6. Fast-paced
7. Dynamic
8. Proven track record
9. Problem solver
10. Entrepreneurial

Just the Facts About Your LinkedIn Profile

➤ Your profile is the place to showcase your skills and experience.

➤ A complete profile includes a professional photo, Executive Summary, skill sets, at least three recent positions, and three recommendations from connections.

Chapter 4

How to Manage Your HomePage

Your LinkedIn HomePage provides the following:

> ➤ News
> ➤ Updates from your network
> ➤ Invitations to connections
> ➤ People you may know
> ➤ Who has viewed your profile
> ➤ Colleagues and classmates that have recently joined

To get to the HomePage, click the LinkedIn logo in the top left corner of every LinkedIn page.

Figure 4-1: Click the LinkedIn Logo in top left corner to go to the HomePage.

The Inbox on the HomePage is your center of communication. With the Inbox, you can:

> ➤ Reply to messages and invitations
> ➤ Delete, archive, flag, or mark messages as read or unread
> ➤ Filter/sort messages by name, subject, or date

> ➤ Compose messages to contacts in your network

Sharing on the HomePage is an easy way to build a network and allow others to know more about you. You can share ideas, articles, questions, and updates. Posts can be visible to anyone or to just connections. Sharing every day helps you build a reputation in your industry.

Remember to click the Twitter box to post you update on your Twitter feed.

The People You May Know feature on the HomePage allows you to grow your network and build professional relationships with others. On the home page, there is a list of suggested people you may know. You can click connect to invite a person to connect on LinkedIn.

Figure 4-2: Invite people you may know to connect to LinkedIn.

You can also remove someone from the People You May Know section or click on a profile to learn more about a person.

How to Make Connections

A connection is a person who is connected to you through LinkedIn. There are three different degrees of how you are connected to people on LinkedIn.

- ➢ First-degree connections are people that you are directly connected to. You know these people personally and these are usually past classmates, colleagues, group members, friends, or family.
- ➢ Second-degree connections are first-degree connections of a first-degree connection. In other words, they are friends of friends.
- ➢ Third-degree connections are first-degree connections of a second-degree connection. In other words, a friend of a friend of a friend.

For example, the member below has 53 first-degree connections. However, after adding up all the network connections of these 53 connections, this member could reach over 7,000 other people on LinkedIn. After adding in all the third-degree connections, this member could reach more than 700,000 members. A list of connections such as these will help you advance your career.

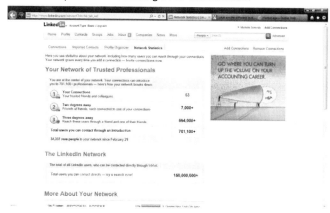

Figure 4-3: Network statistics of a LinkedIn member.

How to Join Groups

By joining groups, you build new relationships with people in your industry or who share your interests. Be sure to join groups that are relevant to you. There are two ways to join groups on LinkedIn.

The first way to join a group is click on the group logo found on the profile of one your first-degree connections. The second way is to search LinkedIn for groups that interest you and then join the group.

To search for groups on LinkedIn, follow these steps:

1. From the top navigation bar, click Group and then select Group Directory.
2. A list of featured groups will appear. You can choose to join one or more of these groups and/or do a search.

3. Enter some keywords in the textbox next to groups.

4. Click the Search button to see a list of groups that match your keywords.

5. To join a LinkedIn group, click the title of the Join Group.

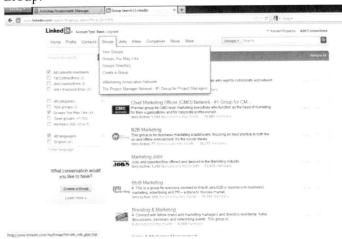

Figure 4-4: Groups are a way to build new relationships with other professionals with similar interests.

Once you join a group, you can share links and news and join discussions. Sharing consistently is a great way to become an expert in your field. As a member of a LinkedIn group, you can like and comment on discussions.

Just the Facts About Your LinkedIn HomePage

- ➢ Your LinkedIn HomePage provides news, updates from your network, invitations to connections, people you may know, who has viewed your profile, and colleagues and classmates that have recently joined.
- ➢ A connection is a person who is connected to you through LinkedIn. There are three different degrees of how you are connected to people on LinkedIn: first-degree connections, second-degree connections, and third-degree connections.
- ➢ By joining groups, you build new relationships with people in your industry or who share your interests. Be sure to join groups that are relevant to you.

Chapter 5

Preparing to Find a Job Using LinkedIn

Before you begin to search for a job using LinkedIn, make sure your profile is up-to-date and complete. The more complete your profile is, the more likely you are to receive job opportunities.

To use LinkedIn to find a job, you should:

- Create a complete profile.
- Add a professional-looking photo.
- Create a professional summary.
- Include keywords and skills in your profile.
- Update your contact settings.
- Provide links to websites and blogs.
- Make your profile public.
- Add a signature.
- Use LinkedIn Answers.
- Build your network.
- Get recommendations from other connections.
- Join your Twitter account to LinkedIn.

Create a Profile

In Chapter 3, we discussed how to create a complete profile. Remember, a complete profile includes a professional-looking photo, professional summary, skill sets, at least three recent positions, and three recommendations from your connections.

Add a Photo

The photo should be professional looking. A headshot photo is best.

Create a Professional Summary

Your professional summary includes your professional experience and goals. Usually this is a one-paragraph summary of recent accomplishments and future goals. Most often the summary is the first place people go on your profile. When writing your professional summary, be concise, be honest, and use keywords.

To create your professional summary, follow these steps:

1. Select Profile from the top navigation bar.
2. Click Edit Profile.
3. Scroll down to Summary and click on Edit.
4. Type your summary.
5. When you have completed your summary, click Save Changes.

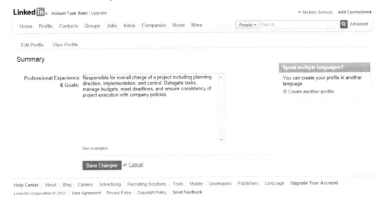

Figure 5-1: Be sure to click Save Changes after you have completed your professional summary.

Include Keywords and Skills in Your Profile

Include all keywords and skills from your resume in your profile. Some potential employers will search for potential applicants by keyword.

Update Your Contact Settings

Before you begin searching for jobs on LinkedIn, make sure your contact settings are up to date. This will let people know what you are available to do.

To update your contact settings, follow these steps:

1. Click Profile from the top navigation bar.

2. Scroll down the page to the bottom of your profile until you Contact "Your Name" For. Click change contact preferences.

3. Select one choice for What type of messages will you accept. Note: Your first-level connections can always send you messages through LinkedIn. If you do not want just anyone sending you messages, make sure you select the "I'll accept only introductions" option.

4. Select the options you want in the Opportunity Preferences section. These will appear in your profile as a bulleted list.

5. Complete the box so people know how to contact you and what type of information you need before you add someone to your network.

6. Click Save Changes.

Figure 5-2: Updating Contact Settings lets other people know what your opportunity preferences are.

Provide Links to Websites and Blogs

In your profile, the Additional Information section allows out to add more information you want people to know. You can add the following:

> ➤ Websites. You can add up to three different website links. These can be links to a blog, your company website, your personal website, or an RSS feed. Always test your links and take a close look to make sure the content is appropriate.

> ➤ Interests. List your interests outside of your job. For example, list your hobbies or sports that you play.

> ➤ Groups and Associations. List any groups or associations you belong to, including charity organizations.

> ➤ Honors and Awards. List any honors or awards you have earned during your career.

To update Additional Information for your profile, follow these steps:

1. Click Profile from the top navigation bar.
2. Scroll down your profile until you see Additional Information and click Edit.
3. Enter up to three website links. First choose which type of website you are linking to, then enter the URL.
4. Complete the Interests box.

5. Complete the Groups and Associations box.
6. Complete the Honors and Awards box.
7. When you have completed the Additional Information page, click Save Changes.

Figure 5-3: The Additional Information profile page allows you to add links to websites, list interests, groups and associations, as well as honors and awards.

Make Your Profile Public

For the purposes of finding a job on LinkedIn, your profile should be public. By making your profile public, your profile will come up in web searches. If you make your profile private, it will not come up in any search engines, thus reducing exposure to your profile and possible job opportunities.

To set your profile to public, follow these steps:

1. Click Profile from the top navigation bar.
2. Click Edit next to Public Profile.
3. You can customize your public profile URL by clicking on the link. Note: Your custom URL must include 5 to 30 letters or numbers. Do not include symbols, spaces, or special characters. Changing your URL frequently will lead to different versions of your profile coming up when someone searches for you on the Internet.
4. You can promote your profile by adding badges. To do this, click Create a profile badge in the Profile Badges box.
5. To control how you appear when people search for you on the Internet, select which section of your profile you want to be public.

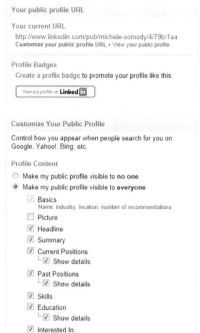

Figure 5-4: Making your LinkedIn profile public increases your visibility on Internet searches.

Create a Signature

You can create your own LinkedIn e-mail signature to increase visibility. To create an e-mail signature, follow these steps:

1. Click Tools at the bottom of your LinkedIn home page.
2. Click Try it Now in the E-mail Signature section.

3. Choose a design from the Select Layout section or click the View Gallery link.

4. Enter your contact information. Whatever information you enter will be included in your signature file.

5. Scroll to the bottom and choose your e-mail program. A pop-up window appears.

6. Choose your e-mail client and follow those instructions. LinkedIn supports all of the most popular e-mail programs.

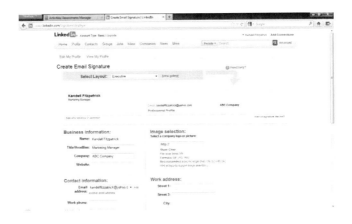

Figure 5-5: Creating a signature increases your visibility.

Use LinkedIn Answers

LinkedIn Answers is a great way to share your business knowledge and expertise and to keep up-to-date on your industry. You ask a question and get answers from your network and other experts. Or, you can show your experience and knowledge by answering questions.

To post a question or answer a question, follow these steps:

1. Click More from the top navigation bar.
2. Select Answers from the drop-down menu.
3. To post a question, enter the question in the Ask a Question box.
4. To answer a question, click Answer Question. You can choose to answer the question or suggest an expert.
5. Note: You can browse questions within a certain category too.

Figure 5-6: Using LinkedIn Answers allows you to share your business knowledge.

When a questioner chooses your answer as the best answer, you earn a point of expertise in the question category. To earn points, answer questions in your area of expertise. The more points you earn, the higher you are on the list of experts.

Note: If you answer a question, it becomes a part of your profile. You can choose to answer a question privately via e-mail.

Build A Network

LinkedIn is a networking site used by professionals to create a network of professionals, search for jobs, and post jobs. Think about why you are joining LinkedIn and how you plan to use the site. Answering these questions will help you in building your network.

Use the invitations, introductions, and InMails tools to build your LinkedIn network. Remember, only connect with trusted individuals.

Get Recommendations from Connections

Ask your direct connections for requests recommendations because they are your most trusted connections.

When someone writes you a recommendation, it comes to you for review (it is not posted). You have the option to accept, reject, or request a revision of the recommendation.

All accepted recommendations are posted on your profile page with links to the profile of the person who wrote the recommendation. This helps validate the recommendation.

Recommendations should be specific, describe exactly what you did, and how it impacted the company/product. There is a 3,000 character limit. Recommendations should say what you want to express and no more.

When asking for a recommendation from a direct connection, include a personal message. Do not use the default message provided by LinkedIn. Be sure to tell the person why you are making the request for a recommendation.

Remember, you need three recommendations to have a complete LinkedIn profile.

To create a recommendation request, follow these steps:

1. Click Profile from the top navigation bar.
2. Select Recommendations from the drop-down menu.
3. Click the Request Recommendations link.
4. Decide what you want to be recommended for by clicking the drop down menu.
5. Decide who you will ask for recommendations. You can view all connections by clicking the LinkedIn button.

6. Create your message. You can change the subject line and edit the message as you request recommendations from each contact. Remember to write a personal message instead of using the default message.
7. Review your recommendation request.
8. Click the Send button to send your request.

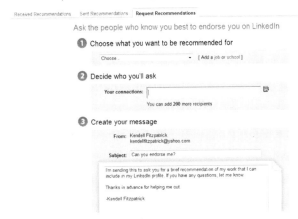

Figure 5-7: LinkedIn recommendations are credible.

You can edit or delete recommendations at any time. To edit or delete a recommendation, follow these steps:

1. Click Profile on the top navigation bar.
2. Click Recommendation from the drop-down menu.
3. Click Edit next to the recommendation you want to edit or delete.

Recommendations that are deleted are removed immediately and no notification is sent to the person who wrote the recommendation.

If you edit a recommendation, it is sent to the person who wrote it for approval.

Recommendations are sent to your LinkedIn inbox. You can choose to accept and show a recommendation on your profile, accept and hide it, request edits to the recommendation, or archive the recommendation.

The more recommendations you have, the better; keep in mind, however, that you want to have high quality recommendations on your profile, as they reflect directly on your work experience and skills.

Linking Your Twitter Account to LinkedIn

By linking your Twitter account to LinkedIn, you provide a broad picture of your professional interests and ideas. It is important to remember that Twitter and LinkedIn are two different types of networks. Twitter is more casual, while LinkedIn is more professional and can be used to further your career. So, think about what you want to share across both networks.

To add your Twitter account to LinkedIn, follow these steps:

1. Click Profile and select Edit Profile from the dropdown menu.
2. Click Add Twitter Account.

Figure 5-8: Join your Twitter account to LinkedIn.

3. Verify your account name and password.

Figure 5-9: Verify your account name and password.

4. Decide how you want to share your tweets on LinkedIn. You have the option to share all tweets or some tweets.

Remember, your Twitter account must be set as public on LinkedIn.

Just the Facts About Using LinkedIn to Find a Job

To use LinkedIn to find a job, you should:

> ➤ Create a complete profile.
> ➤ Add a professional-looking photo.
> ➤ Create a professional summary.

- Include keywords and skills in your profile.
- Update your contact settings.
- Provide links to websites and blogs.
- Make your profile public.
- Add a signature.
- Use LinkedIn Answers.
- Build your network.
- Get recommendations from other connections.
- Join your Twitter account to LinkedIn.

Chapter 6

Finding a Job Using LinkedIn

Gone are the days of finding a job by looking through the classified ads in your local newspaper. One in five employers use social networking sites such as LinkedIn, Twitter, and Facebook to find job candidates. LinkedIn by far dominates the social networking sites for finding qualified job candidates.

There are two main types of job seekers:

1. Active job seekers who need a job now.
2. Passive job seekers who are content with their current job but open to the right job opportunity.

How to Find Jobs on LinkedIn

To find a job on LinkedIn: Click Jobs from the top navigation bar and select Find Jobs from the drop down menu.

This brings you to the Jobs Home page.

A Simple Guide to Finding a Job with LinkedIn

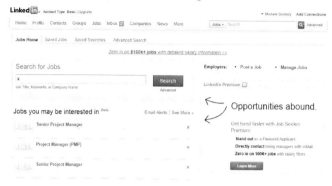

Figure 6-1: The Jobs Home page.

You can do a simple job search by searching for jobs by job title, keywords or company name. For example, Figure 6-2 shows a job search by job title, Marketing Manager.

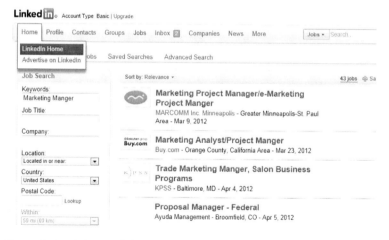

Figure 6-2: A job search by job title.

You can refine your search by:

➢ Relationship

➢ Company

➢ Location

➢ Date posted

➢ Salary

➢ Job function

➢ Industry

➢ Experience level

Refine by Relationship

Refining your search by relationship allows you to search by all relationships, including 1st degree connections, 2nd degree connections, 3rd degree connections and Everyone Else. Select which degree of relationship you want to search by and a new list of job searches are displayed.

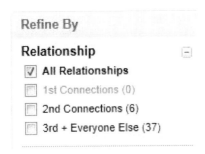

Figure 6-3: A job search refined by relationship type.

Refine by Company

Refining your search by company allows you to search by a specific company or set of companies. Select All Companies to show all job listings, or you can select a specific company. You can also perform a search by typing in a specific company name in the search box.

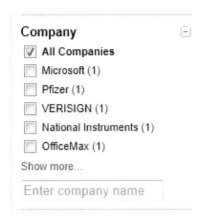

Figure 6-4: A job search refined company.

Refine by Location

Refining your search by location allows you to search for a job listing by in a specific geographic location. Select All Locations to show all job listings, or select a specific city or country from the list. You can also perform a search by typing in a specific location in the search box.

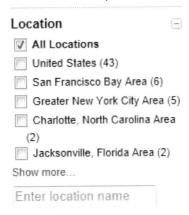

Figure 6-5: A job search refined by location.

Refine by Date Posted

Refining your search by date posted allows you to search for a job listing by the date the job was posted. Select Any Time to show all job listings, or select a specific time period.

Figure 6-6: A job search refined by date posted.

Refine by Salary

Refining your search by salary allows you to search for a job listing by a particular salary range. Select All Salary Levels to show all job listings, or select a specific Salary Level to show only those jobs in that salary range. Note: Salary information is provided by PayScale. It is based on job-specific attributes. Actual compensation may vary by company. All salaries are based on the United States dollar.

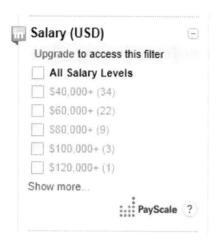

Figure 6-7: A job search refined by salary.

Refine by Job Function

Refining a search by job function allows you to pinpoint listings by job function. Select All Job Functions to show all job listings, or select a specific job function to show only those jobs in that function.

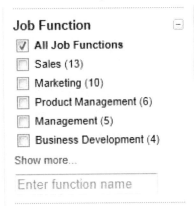

Figure 6-8: A job search refined by job function.

Refine by Industry

Refining your search by industry allows you to dial in to job listings by industry. Select All Industries to show all job listings, or select a specific industry to show only those jobs in that industry.

Figure 6-9: A job search refined by industry.

Refine by Experience Level

Refining your search by experience level lets you specify the amount of job experience you want to search on. Select All Experience Levels to show all job listings, or select an experience level to show only those jobs in that level.

Figure 6-10: A job search refined by experience level.

Search by Relevance

Once you have done a search, you can sort by Relevance, including:

> ➢ Relationship
> ➢ Date Posted (most recent)
> ➢ Date Posted (earliest)

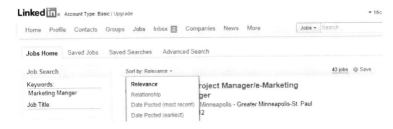

Figure 6-11: You can sort by relevance.

View Job Details

To view the job details about a particular position at a company, click on the job title.

Figure 6-12: Click on the position to view job details.

The job details page provides a job description, company description, and additional information.

The job description includes a description, responsibilities, required skills, experience, and much more.

Job Description

The engineering culture at LinkedIn is based on building and integrating cutting-edge technologies while encouraging creativity, innovation, and expansion. Our engineers constantly raise the bar for excellence, motivating each other to tackle challenges and take intelligent risks. The industry is moving fast and our engineers are right there with it! http://engineering.linkedin.com/

We're proud of our distributed Java applications capable of serving billions of page views to over 130 million LinkedIn members across browsers, iPads, iPhones, Android and Blackberry phones.
With our site experiencing dramatic growth, we are seeking engineers to contribute to massively scaling LinkedIn.

Responsibilities
§ Analyze large scale distributed environments and find system wide bottlenecks within our production environment.
§ Drive overall technical effort to meet LinkedIn's performance objectives
§ Evangelize performance best practices across the company.
§ Build state of the art tools that analyze large volumes of performance data to predict potential performance issues.

Required Skills and Experience
§ Industry leading experience in Performance Analysis, modeling and optimization at internet scale.
§ Experience from processor architecture, storage and interconnect technologies, to large scale distributed applications running on these systems.
§ Strong mentorship skills with the ability to come up with and evangelize Best Practices both within and outside the Performance Team.
§ MS or PhD in Computer Science

Preferred Skills and Experience
§ Ability to support multiple test and performance environments.
§ Ability to triage issues in order to keep software deployments running
§ Experience in debugging browser side issues
§ Exceptionally strong algorithmic problem solving skills

Figure 6-13: A sample job description.

The company description includes basic information. Additional information includes when the job was posted, type of job, level of experience needed, functions, industry, and identification.

Company Description

Founded in 2003, LinkedIn connects the world's professionals to make them more productive and successful. With more than 150 million members worldwide, including executives from every Fortune 500 company, LinkedIn is the world's largest professional network on the Internet. The company has a diversified business model with revenues coming from member subscriptions, marketing solutions and hiring solutions. Headquartered in Silicon Valley, LinkedIn has offices in 22 countries across the globe.

Additional Information

Posted:	April 9, 2012
Type:	Full-time
Experience:	Not Applicable
Functions:	Engineering
Industries:	Information Technology and Services, Internet
Employer Job ID:	4973
Job ID:	2826553

Apply with **LinkedIn** Apply with Resume

Figure 6-14: A sample company description and additional information.

How to Apply for a Job on LinkedIn

When you see a job you want to apply for, click the "Apply" button on the job's page. Note: The way this button works may vary from job to job. For example, you will be able to apply for some jobs directly with LinkedIn, other jobs will direct you to the company's website.

Figure 6-15: You can apply for a job in many different ways.

Apply with LinkedIn

You can apply for a job directly through LinkedIn. Click the Apply with LinkedIn button. The following pop-up box will appear.

Figure 6-16: You can apply for a job through LinkedIn.

Be sure to include your e-mail address and telephone number. To add a cover letter, click Add Cover Letter. There is a default cover letter, but it is suggested that you personalize the letter to explain why you are qualified for the job. When you have completed the cover letter, click Submit Application. Once you click Submit, your full profile will be sent to LinkedIn.

Apply with Resume

You can also apply for a job with a resume. Click Apply with Resume and the following screen will appear.

A Simple Guide to Finding a Job with LinkedIn

| Insert a Resume | Information will automatically be inserted in the fields below. |

Apply with LinkedIn

First Name:*

Last Name:*

Email:*

LinkedIn Profile:*

Field of Interest for Software Engineer Applicants:
- [ ] Software Application Development
- [ ] Systems and Infrastructure
- [ ] Data Analysis, Data Mining and Machine Learning
- [ ] Tools Engineers
- [ ] Mobile
- [ ] Performance Engineer
- [ ] Front End Engineers
- [ ] Open to all Engineering opportunities

Field of Interest for Software Engineers in Test Applicants:
- [ ] Release QA
- [ ] Software Engineer in Test
- [ ] Open to all Engineering opportunities

Optional Information:

Phone:

Cell Phone:

Cover Letter: Insert a document (optional)

Resume:*   Insert a document

Spell Check

Additional Attachments: Add an Attachment

U.S. Equal Employment Opportunity/Affirmative Action Information

Individuals seeking employment at LinkedIn are considered without regards to race, color, religion, national origin, age, sex, marital status, ancestry, physical or mental disability, veteran status, or sexual orientation. You are being given the opportunity to provide the following information in order to help us comply with federal and state Equal Employment Opportunity/Affirmative Action record keeping, reporting, and other legal requirements.

Please Note: Completion of this form is voluntary

Completion of the form is entirely voluntary. Whatever your decision, it will not be considered in the hiring process or thereafter. Any information that you do provide will be recorded and maintained in a confidential file.

Gender:

- Male
- Female
- Decline to Self Identify

Ethnicity:

- Hispanic or Latino - A person of Cuban, Mexican, Puerto Rican, South or Central American, or other Spanish culture or origin, regardless of race.

Race:

- White - A person having origins in any of the original peoples of Europe, the Middle East, or North Africa.
- Black or African American - A person having origins in any of the Black racial groups of Africa.
- Native Hawaiian or Other Pacific Islander - A person having origins in any of the original peoples of Hawaii, Guam, Samoa, or other Pacific Islands.
- Asian - A person having origins in any of the original peoples of the Far East, Southeast Asia, or the Indian subcontinent including, for example, Cambodia, China, India, Japan, Korea, Malaysia, Pakistan, the Philippine Islands, Thailand, and Vietnam
- American Indian or Alaska Native - A person having origins in any of the original peoples of North and South America (including Central America), and who maintains tribal affiliation or community attachment.
- Two or More Races - All persons who identify with more than one of the above races.
- Decline to Self Identify

[Submit Application]

Figure 6-17: You can apply for a job with a resume through LinkedIn.

Complete the application. Any information with an asterisk (*) is required information.

When you apply via the company's website, LinkedIn will re-direct you to the company website. The application process for each company is different. Be sure to read carefully and follow directions.

Top Things NOT to Do on LinkedIn

When using LinkedIn to help you find a job, there are certain things that you definitely should NOT do!

1. Remember that this is a business opportunity. Don't link to your personal Facebook/Twitter/social networking sites… Be professional!

2. Use LinkedIn wisely. Reaching out to recruiters can be done, but in a respectful way. Most won't have time to review your resume, so if you do approach a recruiter, make sure you have a specific question about a post. This way, you'll have a better chance of getting a reply. Asking directly for the e-mail address or phone number of a prospective employer is usually not a good move.

3. Put forth your "professional self" on your profile page. Use professional photos, not personal ones or ones including other people.

4. Don't connect with everyone! The primary point of LinkedIn is to "connect" with others in your field of work. Be careful with your connections: Do you know them personally? Did you do business together? Are they involved in your industry? Remember, LinkedIn is not Facebook and should not be treated as a social site.

5. Stay away from overused words. When describing your past positions and abilities, be creative. Don't be like everyone else. The top five most commonly used phrases on LinkedIn are: creative, organizational, effective, extensive experience, and track record. Stay away from these phrases!

6. Trading recommendations. If all of your recommendations come from people whom you've also recommended, recruiters may believe you and your

friends are simply swapping endorsements. And recruiters do check this!

7. Remember to update your profile. An updated, well-designed profile is key when trying to appeal to recruiters. Not only should your previous work experience be listed in an organized manner, but your current position should also be included. Companies don't want to guess where you work.

8. Stay involved with "Groups." LinkedIn groups were created to benefit users, so stay social and participate in applicable forums. Search for groups in your field of work and in your general location for the most targeted results. Also, be aware of recruiters that may reach out to specific forums and join in.

9. Use your real name in the Profile Name field. Don't use your e-mail. It will throw off LinkedIn's search option.

Northport-East Northport Public Library

To view your patron record from a computer, click on
the Library's homepage: www.nenpl.org

You may:
- request an item be placed on hold
- renew an item that is overdue
- view titles and due dates checked out on your card
- view your own outstanding fines

**151 Laurel Avenue
Northport, NY 11768
631-261-6930**